HOME SERIES

HOME SERIES
SEASIDE LIVING

BETA-PLUS

CONTENTS

P. 4-5
This Villa in Ramatuelle was designed by the architect Mouniguet and converted by Christel de Vos (De Vos Projects).

P. 6
Nik Karalis (Woods Bagot Architects) designed this beach house – located off the coast of St-Andrews beach, Victoria – which respects and preserves the natural landscape.

INTRODUCTION

S easide living: is it the ideal way to live? Living everyday life on the waterfront is without doubt an undeniable privilege. In tribute to the scenery to be found outdoors, the interiors of the seaside houses presented in this volume offer contemporary interior design and architecture that allows the beauty of different landscapes to be expressed under no uncertain terms. More so than any other type of house, the conception, design and layout of the seaside house is determined by the very nature which surrounds it.

The architecture of the seaside house is characterised by spaces which have been given over to daily contemplation. Opening up to the sea, these houses built in pure lines, with vast picture windows, sublimate the landscape in a quest for absolute light. This markedly modern effect is often combined with a deliberately refined interior design; furniture with striking, simple, ultra-contemporary lines and modest shapes, which reduce as much as possible any visual annoyance.

The omnipresent sea dictates the tone of these living spaces: most of the buildings presented here show an abundance of glass, of natural and simple materials and monochrome colours for a dialogue which is permanent and balanced between exterior and interior, nature and architecture.

P. 8
The sunny terrace of an apartment designed by Marc Corbiau and decorated by Annick Colle. From the dark wood director's chairs, which are surrounded by American beachgrass dunes, a magnificent view of the sea can be enjoyed.

P. 10-11
This project by Stefan Antoni/Saota Architects is located in the surroundings of the Cape. The thatch-roofed building pictured was recently renovated and given a new, decisively modern look.

ON THE WATERFRONT

E stablished in the hollow of a valley, stretching out towards the sea, three successive flat roof terraces complete the living spaces of this building, which open out widely onto the landscape. The exterior surroundings are intended to be immaterial: wide picture windows between the horizontal open spaces create both flooring and roofing.

The structure punctuates the interior of the building to form the layout of the different rooms. Further away, an envelope created by an immense wall, which is built up over three levels, is pierced by several very narrow, vertical windows, which definitively anchor the stone construction.

From the entranceway located on the upper level, the gift of light grows gradually on discovery of the rest of the building. Bodies of water, terraces and swimming pools suffice to form an on-site foreground, which is the only obvious design feature of this house designed by the architect Bruno Erpicum.

Wide picture windows between the horizontal open spaces.

The house nestles into the hillside.

The main entranceway is built around a patio, which is finished with an ornamental pool.

The fluidity of the spaces, which are arranged on different levels, is amplified by several staircases that connect each of the bedrooms.

The vast roofing cantilever provides shade for the terrace that leads off the master bedroom, which opens up widely onto the bay.

A canopy elaborated by the architect completes the terrace which leads off the master bedroom.

The pool-house is located underneath the middle terrace.

P. 16-17
Three successive flat roof terraces, which open out extensively onto the landscape, complete the living spaces.

The ground floor living room is arranged around an open fireplace, a cascading view of which can be seen from the dining room on the first floor.

The kitchen and the dining room are arranged on the middle floor, with an "anteroom" positioned between each. The table and consoles were designed by the architect.

Note...

> The sliding walls, in walnut, add a sense of rhythm to the space, accentuating the graphics of the room and creating obvious modularity.

The kitchen is organised around a central island.

The sliding patio doors open up completely, transforming the bedroom into a kind of covered terrace.

Decoration idea

> The mirror in the bathroom, with its pure lines, is nonetheless original: the three strips into which it is cut add rhythm.

> Despite being an open space, the wood panels on the walls and on the floor around the bed delineate and visually frame the sleeping area, thus emphasising it.

The master bedroom has an en-suite bathroom and a living room-cum-library. These rooms are separated from the bedroom by the anterooms, which are revealed on opening the sliding panels.

The main bathroom offers two basins, which are positioned around a central console table.

A RENOVATED HOLIDAY VILLA

ON THE BAY OF SAINT-TROPEZ

T his villa on the bay of Saint-Tropez was designed in 1950 by Raymond Louis, who is as much reputed for being a designer as an architect.

His most famous design works include the Coca-cola bottle and the Shell logo.

Over the past few years, this holiday home – with its superb location – has been transformed and extended by the Belgian architect Michel Lesot. The interior layout was assigned to Gilles de Meulemeester (Ebony Interiors). The kitchen is a creation by Zen Design of Saint-Tropez.

The vast teak decking overlooks the bay and provides a continuously changing view.

P. 26-27
The teak steps were added during the recent renovation.

The natural beige stone "Antalya Cream" was selected for all of the rooms. Most of the decorations in the house are red, which, against the beige of the stone, is the dominant colour.

Note...

> The combination of red and white is a design concept which is uniform because it is expressed and scrupulously respected throughout the entire living space.
The immaculate whiteness dramatises the interior design, creating complete purity which is set off and revitalised by several flashes of red magenta, which add structure to the space.

P. 30-31

The sofas, finished in white cotton, are part of a collection by Tacchini. All of the soft furnishings were supplied by Ebony, as well as the living room table (Artelano) and the stand-up lamps (Modénature).

The chairs, banquettes and lamps were made to measure by Ebony.

The fuchsia artwork in the background is by Michel Mouffe.

The kitchen was designed by Zen Design of Saint-Tropez.

The natural stone Antalya Cream has
also been used in the bathroom. The
wall lamps are by Liaigre. The bathroom
fittings are by Dornbracht.

Decoration idea

> Painting one wall in a single colour of your choice in the place of a headboard will transform and personalise your bedrooms without stifling them.

Lively, chromatic variations of pastel
tones and orange dominate the other
bedrooms. In contrast, the bathrooms
are plain and practically monochrome.

A CONTEMPORARY LIVING BLOCK

A renowned company in the world of home furnishings, Collection Privée has offices in Cannes and in Valbonne. The company also has an architecture and an interior design conception firm, which is managed by Gilles Pellerin and Nicolette Schouten. The project discussed in this feature is the most recent work undertaken by the architecture firm: it is a powerfully contemporary variation on the typical Provencal villa, and is located on the Côte d'Azur.

Geometrical shapes and symmetry form the basis of the balance of this "living block", which has been designed in a very rigid style.

P. 41-43
Part of the structure has been painted white, and part has been constructed in rough Gneiss rock.

A contemporary interpretation of Provencal "restanque" terraces, the low walls harmoniously integrate the different levels.

The front door is made of zinc.

P. 46-49
The sofas and the living room table are creations by Baltus (Collection Privée). The armchair is by Flexform.

Note...

> Using cool, soothing colours creates a sophisticated, contemporary decor, which adds freshness to particularly simple and airy spaces.

> The see-through wall behind one of the sofas creates a visual interval.

The worktop in the kitchen is finished in Corian. The kitchen units – in grey tinted oak – are made to measure.

Decoration idea

> For a peaceful, relaxed atmosphere in your kitchen, don't place units at a height.

> Choose very large paving stones for flooring to complement the modernity and minimalism of the building.

The main bathroom marries natural Palmyre stone with oak parquet (Cabuy).

Note...

> The perfect balance for a bathroom which is modest and simple, but which still emits warmth, can be created using parquet flooring, painted walls, and by avoiding tiles.

Decoration idea

> Painting window frames black gives an exceptionally striking quality and both frames and emphasises the view.

Note…

> A soft, simple bedroom. The padded headboard adds a touch of luxury.

> The bathroom showcases several natural materials: oak parquet, pebbles, tadelakt, etc.; the perfect combination for a cosy, yet up-to-date feel.

> The shower head is built into the ceiling.

ESPLANADES

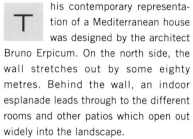

This contemporary representation of a Mediterranean house was designed by the architect Bruno Erpicum. On the north side, the wall stretches out by some eighty metres. Behind the wall, an indoor esplanade leads through to the different rooms and other patios which open out widely into the landscape.

To the south, the continuation of the paved ground and the abundant roofing creates an outer esplanade, which is integrated with the space and built around a natural terrace.

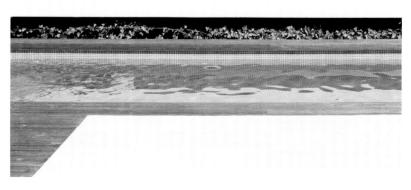

The structure of the building is interrupted to give way to an outdoor dining area.

P. 59-61

To the south, all of the living spaces open up onto the lower terrace. The outer esplanade is devised like the deck of a boat; the sea is visible below the land.

By simply widening the terrace and punctuating it with two pine trees, a patio is created which is integrated with the whole construction.
The outside dining area is finished in gaboon mahogony. The furniture is by Tribu.

The uniform use of colours and materials allows light to seep into every space.

Note...

> Sandblast shades in a whitewashed effect create a calming decor, which is inspired by the colours of the natural environment.

> The ceilings are painted in the same finish so that they blend into the interior design.

The walls and the ceilings are coated with cement, which is largely the same colour as the Calice stone floor. The woodwork elements are finished in natural gaboon mahogony.

The dining room is furnished with two
similar tables, designed by the
architect. The chairs were selected by
S&B Projects.

The master bedroom benefits from a panoramic view, and is finished with a private side terrace.

The bathroom opens out onto the south esplanade. The bath and washstand are in Calice stone.

Decoration idea

> Placing a mirror in a bathroom gives double the mind-blowing view.

A PANORAMIC VIEW

OF THE ISLAND OF FORMENTERA

T his long-abandoned house was acquired by an English couple, who assigned its renovation and transformation to the architect Bruno Erpicum. Its interior design was tasked to the architect Maria Rodriguez Carreno.

A veritable makeover was carried out in order to thoroughly breathe life back into this very colourful building. The esplanade and the exterior spaces were reorganised around a central patio.

The two lower levels have unrestricted access, and were finished with a terrace which finds shade under a sizeable concrete pergola. The sea creates a backdrop to the swimming pool.

Higher up, the bedrooms and their respective terraces show off their size, reminiscent of ancestral fincas.

The raised ground enables the construction of private balcony terraces, which finish each of the bedrooms.

P. 72-73
The balcony terrace off the master bedroom offers a panoramic view across the salt works; in the distance, the island of Formentera can be seen.

An outdoor living space punctuated by three olive trees is an inviting place for a siesta.

The canopy roofing is finished in red; the walls of the central patio are blue.

A staircase leads down to the living room on the lower floor by a sequence of double spaces. The kitchen is found on the upper mezzanine.

Note...

> The spectral chromatic scale which has been selected is uniform: the colour of the wall outside is also used indoors, which merges the outer/inner boundaries.

> The presence of some iconic design pieces, modelled on the mythical Eames Lounge Chair or the Superarchimoon standard lamp by Philippe Starck, adds value to the purified architecture.

A concrete screen wall plays on the lighting and the different levels. The bathroom – a creation by Maria Rodriguez Carreno – is finished in Zimbabwe granite.

THE HOUSE OF NOUREEV

This house was the holiday home of the legendary ballet dancer Rudolphe Noureev, who died in 1993.

A simple building, dating back to the 1950s, the house was constructed on the waterfront of the wild coast of Saint-Barthélemy.

Built against rock, it offers an amazing panorama.

P. 84-91
One of the unique features of this beach house is the sturdy, teak decking.

A heavenly balcony-terrace is suspended over the sea.

The wild coast of Saint-Barth was an ideal setting for inspiring Noureev's creative genius.

The kitchen/dining room. In the photo, opposite, is the piano that was played by the famous Russian dancer for so many years.

Note...

> The interior design is adapted to the environment, and is inspired by the exotic and furnished with indigenous pieces. The atmosphere is relaxed and warm. A particular charm emanates from this interior, which is marked by its simplicity and warmth.

The master bedroom.

THE HORIZON

AS THE ONLY BOUNDARY

N ear the summit of a mountain, between the morning bay window - to the east - and the evening bay window - to the west, a blank wall appears to float between the concrete floor and roof, both of which restrict its movement. If the door is opened for you, the curtain will be raised and you'll find yourself on stage.

Cross the reception area which is made out of wood, go past the dividing wall and then take in the surrounding landscape in all its beauty. The reception areas have a double height; from here, the "sea view" dominates this building, created by architect Bruno Erpicum.

Thereafter, your eyes will constantly be amazed at the discrete yet surprising views which are created through non-portable items being hung up.

Back on the premises where there is a greater degree of privacy, go through an area made of wood which contains all the service rooms and look at the side views which stretch as far as the distant horizon.

A series of screen walls masks the landscape, which is forgotten as you step into the property.

The swimming pool is an infinity pool, which spills over on all four sides; a stone diving board accentuates the reflection of the sky on the pool's surface.

The living areas are open plan.

Decoration idea

> A low wall creates an original perspective, which would welcome and emphasise any work of art.

> The puzzle sofa, which has been positioned in the centre of the room, allows the sea view, the fireplace or library to be fully appreciated.

Decoration idea

> Use the same suspended lighting in the kitchen and dining room for a more harmonious result.

Note...

> The wood wall-tidy extends continuously from the kitchen to the living room.

> The ingenious cubby hole houses the fridge on one side, and features a work of art on the other.

RADICALLY CONTEMPORARY

This house, which is located in Ibiza and was conceived by the architect Bruno Erpicum, is arranged on two levels.

The higher level – a former manege – reminds us that this landscape extends right up to the village. Three entirely separate spaces, which provide shelter over the garage and bedrooms, are all accessible via a double esplanade. This esplanade is emphasised by screen walls, which frame the views and give each respective patio its own privacy.

On the other side is the forest. The living rooms are arranged in a vast space, which gain in height as the ground descends to the lower level. To the left, a huge window reveals the landscape; to the right – further away – the sky is reflected onto the ground by a body of water: this creates a mirror image of the forest. The living room is finished with a stone terrace that leads all the way up to the swimming pool, after which the landscape meets the sea and then the horizon.

The screen walls protect the bedrooms like loyal soldiers; the entrance is at the end of the path.

The ornamental pool announces the living room, which reflects into it, and the kitchen patio receives the morning sun.

The living room is arranged on the lower level.

Note...

> Minimalism is key here; there is no exception to this rule, which highlights all of the structural lines of the furnishings and architecture. The monastic atmosphere allows for complete relaxation of the mind in the soothing, natural environment.

Light, which is reflected by the ornamental pool, adds to the magic of the scene.

The house's furnishings are by the designer Bruno Reymond (la maison de l'Éléphant).

The bedrooms open out onto the garden; the forest and wild flowers are an integral part of the interior design.

HOME SERIES

Volume 30 : SEASIDE LIVING

The reports in this book are selected from the Beta-Plus collection of home-design books: www.betaplus.com
They have been compiled in a special series by Le Figaro in French language: Ma Déco.

Copyright © 2010 Beta-Plus Publishing / Le Figaro
Originally published in French language

PUBLISHER
Beta-Plus Publishing
Termuninck 3
B – 7850 Enghien
Belgium
www.betaplus.com
info@betaplus.com

TEXT
Alexandra Druesne

PHOTOGRAPHY
Jo Pauwels
Jean-Luc Laloux (cover, page 6, page 10 to 23 and 58 to 127)

DESIGN
Polydem - Nathalie Binart

TRANSLATIONS
Txt-Ibis

ISBN : 978-90-8944-084-6

Printed in China

P. 124-127
A view of the sea from 159 m altitude... a project by the architect Bruno Erpicum.